20 Answers

∞

Angels & Demons

By Fr. Mike Driscoll

Catholic Answers Press

20 Answers: Angels & Demons

Fr. Mike Driscoll

© 2016 Catholic Answers

Published by Catholic Answers, Inc.
2020 Gillespie Way
El Cajon, California 92020
1-888-291-8000 orders
619-387-0042 fax
catholic.com

Printed in the United States of America

ISBN 978-1-941663-89-9
ISBN 978-1-941663-90-5 Kindle
ISBN 978-1-941663-91-2 ePub

1. What are angels?

Angels are purely spiritual beings created by God. Strictly speaking, the word *angel* (from the Greek for "messenger") refers to their office, not their nature. In other words, the good spirits who interact with human beings are called angels, whereas those who operate strictly in heaven are more precisely called spirits. However, it is traditional and acceptable to call all of them angels. They are not eternal in the way that God is, that is, existing before and outside of time. Rather, they are eternal in the same way human souls are: once created, they exist forever. Because they do not have bodies, they do not experience the separation of body and soul which we call death.

God used his intellect in conceiving of the universe, and his free will in choosing to create it. Like human beings, angels are created in the image of God, which means they have intellect and free will; they are capable of thought and can choose courses of action. Unlike human beings still on earth, angels do not have to think about what God wants them to do; God enlightens them as to his will, or it may be the case that they consult the divine will as to what should be done (*Summa Theologica* I:107:3). Since seeing the glory of God perpetually gives them happiness to the utmost capacity of their natures, it is impossible for angels not to desire and follow his will.

Being purely spiritual affects the intellectual capabilities of angels in several ways. They do not have emotions as human beings do, so their choices are not influenced by passions such as fear and anger; rather, they act based purely on their intellect. Because the angelic intellect is not physical, i.e., is not connected to a brain, angels do not reason step-by-step to a conclusion as human beings do; instead, they have concepts in mind all at once. For example, when choosing a course of action, angels do not spend time considering different possibilities; they can see all the possibilities at once and immediately make their decision.

Because their knowledge is not limited by physical senses, angels have the ability to know anything that is happening throughout the material world. Should they have the need, angels can intellectually apprehend the temperature at the North Pole, the flow of lava under the earth's crust, or the rate of speed of a distant galaxy hurtling through space. Of course, angels would have no reason to focus their intellect on all such things as they occur, but instead apply their intellect to those things that pertain to God's will for them.

Because angels are purely spiritual beings, they cannot be said to be in a particular place in the same way as a material object. One of God's perfections is that he is present everywhere; in contrast, human beings have bodies, which determine our physical presence. Angels are different from both God and humans: they are not all-present as God is, but they are not connected to bodies as are human beings. Rather, the place where an angel exists at any moment is said to be where it is exerting its power. Angels cannot be in two places at once; in other words, they cannot exert their power in two different places at the same time. But the place where they exert their power need not be a small point; for example, it is just as easy for an angel to be present with a person to give an inspiring thought, as to protect a city, or to change the course of a planet. There are several places in the Bible where angels are described as having wings. Although they can manipulate air and solid matter to take any physical appearance they desire, they remain pure spirit, and so do not actually have wings by nature. The symbolism of wings represents their ability to move from one place to another almost instantaneously.

Time is also different for angels than it is for material beings. Humans comprehend the passage of time by physical means, such as the intellectual capacity of the brain, changes in the body, and the perceptions of the senses. Angels don't use such physical agency, so they do not experience time passing in the same way. The succession of events has meaning for them; in other words, an event succeeds some events and precedes others. But lengths of time do not mean anything to angels: they do not think it has been a long time since God created them, nor a short time. Whether keeping a star in motion for billions of years or speaking for a few minutes to a human being, angels do not tire, do not grow bored, and do not wonder how long until God wills them to do something else.

2. What is the angels' relationship with God?

Whereas God continues to create new human beings, he created all the angels at the beginning of the world. They were all created good, for nothing that God creates is evil, but some rebelled against him, and "rejected God and his reign" (*The Catechism of the Catholic Church* 392). This rebellion was irrevocable: the fallen angels, led by one called Lucifer, are completely evil and never will repent of their sin. Similarly, the angels who chose obedience to God made a permanent choice: none of them would ever decide later to rebel against him. The permanence of the angels' choice is a result of their being pure spirits. We human beings often change our minds about things after gaining further knowledge and seeing the results of our decisions. There are times we make decisions based on heightened emotions and sensual desires, and later—when those influences have calmed—we may repent of a particular choice and make a better one. The angels are different: from the moment God created them, they had all the knowledge they needed to choose good or evil. Unlike us, they do not have senses and emotions that could affect their decisions. Whether an hour or a million years later, nothing in the angels' thinking or experience is different, so the idea of changing their mind does not even make sense to them. Those who rebelled preferred unhappiness to obedience, and nothing they would learn later—not even an eternity of complete misery—would induce them to regret their choice.

What do angels do? Jesus said they constantly behold the face of our heavenly Father; as the *Catechism* states, "The role of the angels is to glorify God without ceasing" (CCC 350). According to St. Thomas Aquinas, the angels carry heaven with them; in other words, they are adoring God no matter where they are. The prophet Isaiah had a vision of angels crying to one another, "Holy, holy, holy is the Lord of hosts; the whole earth is full of his glory" (6:3). At the birth of Christ, after an angel announced the good news to the shepherds, there was a multitude of the heavenly host with the angel, praising God and saying, "Glory to God in the highest, and on earth peace among men with whom he is pleased!" (Luke 2:14). Similarly, the Apostle John had a vision of numerous angels in their worship of the Lamb, i.e., God the Son. And even though they may be in different places, according to St. Thomas, "the angels do not go abroad in such a manner as to lose the delights of inward contemplation" (ST I:112:3). In other words, since their adoration of God is an act of their intellect and will, angels are in continual worship no matter what other action they may be carrying out.

Just as we don't know how many human beings God will create, we also don't know how many angels he created. According to the prophet Daniel, "Thousands upon thousands were ministering to him, and myriads upon myriads stood before him" (7:10). "Myriad" means countless or infinite. Of course there cannot be an infinite number of angels, but this poetic phrase implies there are more than we can imagine. St. Thomas says that because purely spiritual beings are more perfect than material beings, he believes God created incomparably more angels than bodily creatures. In a commonly referenced treatise on angels from the sixth century, a Catholic writer by the magnificent name of Dionysius the Areopagite stated: "There are many blessed armies of the heavenly intelligences, surpassing the weak and limited reckoning of our material numbers."[1] It is mind-boggling to think that the English language (or any other language) does not contain words that could be used to state the number of angels that God has made. For him, it is just as easy to create a number of angels approaching infinity as to create one angel.

3. How do angels interact with one another?

As described by the prophet Isaiah (6:2–3), St. Luke (2:13–14), and St. John (Rev. 4:8), angels' primary interaction with each other consists in their united worship of God. The Bible also describes instances in which a number of angels act together. For example, Abraham's three mysterious visitors were (apparently) angels; they informed him that within a year, his wife Sarah would give birth to a son, despite the couple's advanced age (Gen. 18). Shortly thereafter, two angels appeared to Lot to warn him of the impending destruction of Sodom and Gomorrah (Gen. 19). In the book of the prophet Daniel (ch. 10), there is an enigmatic interplay between an angel assigned to Israel (possibly Gabriel, who is named in ch. 9) and the angel of Persia. The clearest example of both angelic cooperation and resistance on a massive scale is described in the book of Revelation: "Now war arose in heaven, Michael and his angels fighting against the dragon; and the dragon and his angels fought, but they were defeated" (12:7–8). The same book recurrently describes numerous angels taking part in pronouncements and preparations at the end of the world. Jesus, moreover, said that angels will accompany him on Judgment Day (Matt. 16).

Angels do not converse with each other in a human way, since they do not have vocal cords or eardrums with which to talk and hear. But angels do make mental concepts known to one another, and this can be called speech. Superior angels speak to inferior ones to enlighten them about things of God. Inferior angels may speak to superior angels to make known their own interior thoughts, such as, "I wish to learn this from you," or, "God wills that I do that." This illustrates an important point: one angel cannot read the mind of another, for only God knows the thoughts of angels and human beings. A fascinating corollary is that not all angels know when one speaks, but only those being spoken to. Since their speech is purely mental—one mind communicating with another—it is not as if angels converse with audible voices that others can hear. Another consequence of angelic speech being mental is that distance does not affect it: in relation to the material world, angels who are light years apart from one another communicate just as easily as if they were side by side.

Are some angels superior to others? Keeping in mind that the powers of angels are their intellect and will, if some angels are superior to others, their superiority must be through their greater intellect and more powerful will. Since all angels have an equal ability to know the material universe, any differences in intellect must consist in the fact that some were given to understand more deeply the mind of God. St. Thomas Aquinas believed that superior angels sometimes enlighten inferiors on things related to God, but this would not result in equality between them, since the superior would understand the knowledge more deeply. St. Thomas also believed that when acting on behalf of a superior angel, the inferior angel had the power of their superior. He gives the example of an inferior angel using the power of a superior to drive off a demon that would otherwise be too powerful. This implies that the angels are superior and inferior not only in their intellect, but also in the strength of their will. The same truth may also be seen in cases of fallen angels possessing a human being: some demons seem more difficult to drive out than others.

It is believed that angels differ from one another more than human beings differ from one another. In the animal world, each species may have many individuals, whether lobsters, llamas, or human beings. This is due to the fact that animals have physical bodies, so the nature of each species is the same in every member of that species: every lobster has the same lobster nature, every llama has the same llama nature, and every human has the same human nature. But angels do not have bodies, so they have no common nature. In other words, one angel does not differ from another angel as one lobster differs from another lobster, but as a lobster differs from a llama. Or as St. Thomas said more elegantly, as one star differs from another in glory, all the more do angels differ from one another.

4. What is the angels' relationship with us?

Although they have no material form in themselves, angels may, for the sake of human beings with whom they interact, take on a physical appearance by controlling the elements around them. They can do this by manipulating physical elements such as air, sunlight, and the dust of the earth. Such angelic appearances, though truly physical, do not constitute living bodies. Angels may also communicate through visions, in which there is no actual physical appearance, as in St. Joseph's dream and the vision of St. John described in the book of Revelation. Angels also have the ability to give us ideas and inspirations, just as other human beings do; the difference is that angels do so in a nonverbal way.

Angels cannot see the future as God can, though they may sometimes appear to us to do so in two ways. First, God may reveal future events to them as he did to the prophets, which the angels may in turn proclaim to human beings (e.g., the destruction of Sodom and Gomorrah in Genesis 18–19, or the births of John the Baptist and of Jesus in Luke 1). Second, because they are capable of focusing their attention on any external events occurring in the world, angels can predict many events that human beings cannot. For example, someone's guardian angel may know of a dangerous situation that the person cannot see, and may give him an inspiration to avoid the danger. The angel does not see the future, but does have a wider view of events that may affect the person.

Neither angels nor human beings can read hearts and minds as God can. But just as humans can sometimes guess what others are thinking or feeling by nonverbal signs such as body language or facial expression, so angels can do the same. Because they can see more subtle signs and know people more thoroughly through long observation, angels are much better at inferring their thoughts and emotions.

Angels have great power in regard to the material universe. When moving an object in the physical world, angels do not use physical exertion, for they do not have physical bodies. Rather, they move things by a simple act of the intellect and will, and therefore it takes no more strength for an angel to move a planet than to move a peanut. Angels can also manipulate physical matter in more subtle ways. As Moses looked on, an angel made a bush appear to be burning without being consumed. An angel cooled the inside of the fiery furnace where three Israelites (Shadrach, Meshach, and Abednego) had been thrown for refusing to worship a gold statue; they emerged unscathed. St. Peter's guardian angel tapped his shoulder, made light appear in his prison cell, made the chains fall off his wrists, and led him through locked doors and iron gates. These examples illustrate not only angels' power over the material world, but also their role in protecting human beings.

Angels occasionally deliver messages to people, and (as noted previously) the word angel means *messenger*. Well-known angelic messages in the Bible include those to Isaiah (6:7), Manoah and his wife (Judg. 13), Zechariah (Luke 1:1–25), and of course Mary (Luke 1:26–38), Joseph (Matt. 1:18–21), and the shepherds (Luke 2:8–14). People should not be too quick to believe that an angel is speaking to them, but at the same time Catholics should not deny the possibility.

It would be a mistake to think of angels only as servants of human beings, for as God has appointed them to serve us, he also assigns them to carry out his judgment. After Adam and Eve sinned, God expelled them from the garden of Eden; in a mysterious reference, Genesis says that "at the east of the garden of Eden" God "placed the cherubim, and a flaming sword which turned every way, to guard the way to the tree of life" (3:24). When the Assyrians were about to invade Jerusalem, God answered the prayer of the Israelite King Hezekiah and sent one angel who killed 185 thousand enemy soldiers. In his parable of the weeds and the wheat, Jesus described the role of the angels at the end of the world: "The Son of Man will send his angels, and they will gather out of his kingdom all causes of sin and all evildoers, and throw them into the furnace of fire; there men will weep and gnash their teeth" (Matt. 13:41–42).

On a brighter note, it is helpful for Catholics at Mass to keep in mind that angels are present, assisting the priest. In the extraordinary form of the Mass, while he incenses the bread and wine, the priest prays:

"Through the intercession of blessed Michael the arch-angel standing at the right hand of the altar of incense, and of all his elect, may the Lord vouchsafe to bless this incense and to receive it in the odor of sweetness." The Roman Canon, also known as Eucharistic Prayer I, includes this request: "In humble prayer we ask you, almighty God, command that these gifts be borne by the hands of your holy angel to your altar on high." In the Byzantine Liturgy, the Cherubic Hymn reminds the faithful that angels surround the body of Christ:

We who mystically represent the cherubim,
and who sing to the life-giving Trinity the
    thrice-holy hymn,
let us now lay aside all earthly cares
that we may receive the King of all,
escorted invisibly by the angelic orders. Alleluia.

5. Where do we get names for angels and angel choirs?

Angels do not use names amongst themselves in the sense of informing one another of who they are, since they know one another through mental concepts. However, in the Bible there are four angels who have names associated with their identity or function. The leader of the fallen angels is addressed by several names: Satan, the name by which Jesus refers to him several times, means *enemy* or *adversary*; Beelzebul, another term Jesus used, comes from a derogatory name for a god of the Canaanites and means *lord of the flies*; and Lucifer, a metaphorical reference to the king of Babylon (Isa. 14:12), means *light-bearer* or *morning star*, reminding us that the devil is a fallen angel. In regard to the good angels, the name Michael means *who is like unto God*: this was Michael's response to the devil's declaration, "I will be like God." Michael appears in the books of Daniel, Jude, and Revelation. Gabriel means *God is my strength*; he is also in the book of Daniel, and (of course) in Luke's Gospel. Raphael may be translated *God heals*; he is a key personage in the book of Tobit. We also see in Scripture that angels do not always reveal their names. On one occasion Menoah, father of Samson, asked an angel its name; the angel replied, "Why do you ask my name, seeing it is wonderful?" (Judg. 13:18). Concerning the fallen angels, the Rite of Exorcism instructs the exorcist to ask the name of the possessing evil spirits. Exorcists say these demons resist giving their names, because doing so gives the exorcist more authority over them. But the possessing demons are forced to reveal their names when the exorcist repeatedly invokes the more powerful name of Jesus.

The names of nine different groups or "choirs" are found in Scripture and in the Mass, but there is nothing in Scripture or in Church doctrine that specifies what these different names imply about the actual differences between the choirs. St. Thomas Aquinas, St. Gregory the Great, and Dionysius the Areopagite organized the nine choirs into three groups, or hierarchies, according to the depth of their knowledge and understanding of God. The first hierarchy consists of seraphim, cherubim, and thrones; the second of dominions, virtues, and powers; the third of principalities, archangels, and angels.

Seraphim means *fiery ones*, referring to their burning love of God; they are mentioned in the Bible just once, in the book of Isaiah. Cherubim means *winged messenger*; they are mentioned several times in the Old Testament, as when God instructed Moses to build the Ark of the Covenant with winged cherubim made of gold on the lid.

The choirs of angels are mentioned in St. Paul's letter to the Ephesians, in which he describes Jesus as "far above all rule and authority and power and dominion, and above every name that is named, not only in this age but in the age to come" (1:21). This list is similar to that found in Paul's letter to the Colossians, in his beautiful explanation of Jesus as the second person of the Triune God: "He is the image of the invisible God, the first-born of all creation; for in him all things were created, in heaven and on earth, visible and invisible, whether thrones or dominions or principalities or authorities—all things were created through him and for him" (1:15–16).

The word "archangel" is found twice in the Bible, both times in the New Testament. Paul says that the end of the world will be signaled by the call of an (unnamed) archangel (1 Thess. 4:16), and St. Jude (verse 9) refers to Michael as an archangel. The last choir, simply called angels, are mentioned dozens of times throughout the Bible, including numerous references by Jesus.

6. What are demons?

Demons are purely spiritual beings created in the image of God. As such they possess intellect and free will, as do human beings; unlike humans, they have no physical body, never grow old, and never die. God created all angels good, but some made a free and permanent decision to disobey and reject him. The creature known as Satan, or Lucifer, is the leader of these evil spirits. He is also called the devil, and the angels who followed him in rejecting God are called devils or demons. Both these English words come from the Latin *diabolus*, meaning *attacker, slanderer,* or *accuser.* This connotation is seen in the words of Jesus, who called the devil a murderer, a liar, and the father of lies (John 8:44), and in the book of Revelation, when the devil is driven from heaven and a celestial voice cries, "The accuser of our brethren has been thrown down" (12:10). At the time of creation, Lucifer may have been the closest to God of all the angels; therefore it may have been a sin of pride that was his definitive act of disobedience. A figurative reading of the prophet Isaiah supports this idea: "How you are fallen from heaven, O day star . . . You said in your heart, 'I will ascend to heaven . . . I will make myself like the Most High'" (14:12–14).

Although the proportion of angels who joined in this rebellion is unknown, a metaphorical reading of the book of Revelation (12:3–4) suggests that one third of all the angels fell. Revelation 12:7–9 also declares that war broke out in heaven, and that Michael and his angels drove out Satan and his angels. It is a little frightening to note that the fallen angels were not confined to hell: "Satan, the deceiver of the whole world—he was thrown down to the earth, and his angels were thrown down with him" (12:9). Their counterparts, the good angels, are said to carry heaven with them even while operating in the material world: Jesus said they constantly behold the face of the heavenly Father (Matt. 18:10). The exact opposite is true of the fallen angels. In some sense they are constantly in hell: even while roaming the earth, they carry hell with them. St. Thomas Aquinas says that the source of their misery is their undying opposition to the will of God, and since they are intelligent enough to see that all things conform to God's will, they are in eternal wretchedness and despair.

The Catholic belief that demons are fallen angels seems quite basic, but it was questioned at one time in Church history. A false teaching known as the Cathar or Albigensian heresy, which was alive from the twelfth to the fourteenth century, held that Satan and the evil spirits are inherently evil. The Fourth Lateran Council (1215) was compelled to reiterate the belief that the demons were created good by God, but became evil when they sinned of their own free will. In the sixteenth century, the *Catechism of the Council of Trent* repeated the biblical descriptions of the nature and work of demons: they are evil, hateful, powerful, and numerous; they tempt human beings to sin, in order to deprive them of heaven; and prayer can be a strong defense against their works (part IV, petition 6). *The Catechism of the Catholic Church* mentions other details: it is not a lack of God's mercy, but the nature of their evil choice, that renders them forever evil; they can harm human beings both spiritually and physically; and it is a mystery why God allows them to continue to afflict human beings (391–395). Their days are numbered, and when Jesus returns for Judgment Day, they will be confined forever to the fires of hell.

Whereas the demons' sin against God consisted in pride and disobedience, their sin against human beings is envy: if they cannot have the happiness of heaven, they prefer that human beings also be deprived of it. Since sin can keep us from heaven, demons continuously tempt us to sin; they are the perpetual, mortal enemies of the human race.

7. What powers do demons have?

Human beings have inherent abilities, sometimes called faculties or powers. For example, humans have intellect and will, sight and the other senses, and body parts which they can move. The use of these various human powers is dependent on the working of the physical body (what happens after death is a different and more mysterious matter). For example, those with brain damage may not have the use of their intellect and will, those whose eyes do not function cannot see, and those without legs cannot walk. At the end of the world, God will miraculously restore to every person a risen body which he will have for eternity, with all of its powers operating properly. A human being is still a human being even if, in this life, he loses the use of his powers.

Because they have no physical bodies, angels are quite different; they essentially have two powers, the intellect and the will. This actually makes them more powerful than humans rather than less so, for they perceive things without the use of the senses, can move from one place to another without the use of limbs, and can move material objects without physical exertion. But they would not be angels if they did not have the use of their intellect and will, which are the powers that constitute the image of God in angels (as well as in human beings). This explains why God does not annihilate the fallen angels, i.e., make them cease to exist. Intellect and will are inherently good, godlike powers, so he does not wipe them out of existence even when they are misused by angels and humans.

How do the demons use these faculties for evil? First, because they can manipulate physical matter, devils can appear to perform miracles. For example, as a rebuttal to the miracles God worked through Moses, Pharaoh's sorcerers appeared to turn their staffs into snakes and water into blood (Exod. 7:8–13). Human beings do not possess these abilities on their own, but this is the kind of deception the devil would perform through a witch or sorcerer in order to draw people away from God.

Another way in which the demons misuse their power is by manipulating physical matter to cause death and disease in human beings. The Old Testament describes the devil causing a powerful wind to collapse a house, killing Job's children, as well as causing severe boils that covered Job's body. The Gospels describe demons causing people to be deaf, blind, and mute; again, they have the power to do this by subtly afflicting the person's body.

A third way the demons misuse their faculties is by combining their acute powers of observation with their ability to give ideas to human beings. Demons can give humans the impression that they (the humans) can read minds and see the future. This was the type of deception that was being performed by a slave girl in the Acts of the Apostles; until St. Paul performed an exorcism, her masters were profiting from her fortune-telling ability. To give a modern example, suppose a demon knows that I am feeling dejected about the death of a friend last week. Suppose I go to a psychic, hoping to learn something about where my friend's soul is now. The demon knows about the death and observes that I am feeling very down today. He can put the idea into the psychic's mind that I am sad over the recent death of my friend. Though the psychic has never met me, he is able to tell me how I am feeling and why. The psychic and I both think he is somehow reading my mind and my feelings, when actually we are both just being used and deceived by the devil.

Consider another example: by knowing my personal habits and listening to my conversations today, a demon may have a good idea of some of the things I will be doing tomorrow. Through his own observations or through communication with another demon, he may also know the plans of another person. I may not realize that I am likely to meet that person tomorrow, but the demons may know that our separate plans will result in our being in the same place at the same time.

Now suppose I were to go to a palm reader today. The demon may put in the palm reader's mind the name of the person I am going to meet tomorrow and the likely circumstances of our encounter. The palm reader thinks he is predicting the future, but he is actually just being used by the devil. When the encounter takes place tomorrow, I too may think the palm reader predicted the future, in which case I too would be deceived by the devil.

8. What are some misconceptions about demons?

From ancient folklore to modern movies, misconceptions about demons spread and persevere. One such misconception is that the devil can read our minds. Only God knows our thoughts, but demons have a particularly frightening ability to observe and remember all of our personal habits. By way of comparison, consider two people who know one another well. When they talk to one another, they know more of what is on the other's mind than is actually said, because they notice tone of voice, facial expressions, and body language. Demons, with their greater intelligence, memory, and powers of observation, are much better at this than any human being. Therefore, even though God alone knows all of our thoughts, demons can make good guesses as to what we are thinking and feeling.

The idea that some people go to hell as a result of selling their souls to the devil is an old, entertaining, and frightening theme of stories. Such tales sometimes convey the false belief that once people make such pacts, they are doomed to eternal damnation. The stories usually involve the devil agreeing to give people power or money, but returning at the end of their lives to drag their souls kicking and screaming into hell. Certainly, asking the devil for assistance of any kind is a mortal sin and, if not repented of, can indeed land a person's soul in the everlasting fire. What must be kept in mind is that as long as people are in this life, they can always repent of their sins and save their souls. Even dealings with the devil may be repented of: it is not unusual for people who consort with evil spirits at some point in their lives to later turn to Jesus Christ for his forgiveness and his gift of salvation.

A similar—if more bizarre—mistake is the thought that demons can in some way physically seize souls and take them to hell. Although this makes for exciting movies, it does not make theological sense. The only way for people to go to hell is by knowingly and willingly breaking God's law in serious matters. There are no physical gateways to hell in haunted places, through which unwitting innocents may stumble, never to return. Although such an error may not be commonly held, there is a widespread misconception that the opposite is true. Priests are regularly asked to bless houses where frightening occurrences have taken place; unfortunately, the residents sometimes seem to think the blessing is of greater importance than living a good moral life. It is absolutely false that a particular ritual or blessing is all that is needed to keep a person safe from hell.

Another mistake worth noting here is the overemphasis on the devil as the cause of sins. A 1970s actor used the phrase "the devil made me do it" in his effective comedy routine, but the belief is not good theology. Certainly the devil is always looking for opportunities to trip us, and in Jesus' parable about those who receive his teachings and later reject them, the devil was indeed one of the causes. But Jesus also said that setbacks, persecutions, worldly anxiety, and the love of money can corrupt people's hearts. A document approved by Pope St. John Paul II calls it a spiritual deviation "when the daily events of life, which have nothing or little to do with our . . . journey toward Christ, are read schematically, indeed childishly, so as to ascribe all setbacks to the devil" ("Directory on Popular Piety and the Liturgy," 2001).

Related to this, a peculiar spirituality has developed amongst some Catholics based on the idea that sins, physical ailments, and mental or emotional disorders can be traced to particular categories of demons. As part of this spirituality, people address the devil directly using dramatic language, for example: "Demon of anger, in the name of Jesus Christ, I renounce you, I bind you, and I send you to the foot of the cross." It is true that demons can cause the entire gamut of physical, mental, emotional, and spiritual problems; that certain demons may indeed have a proclivity to cause certain types of evils; and that individuals should renounce both the devil and their own sins. Where this relatively new practice may lead people astray is in its emphasis on demons as the source of every human struggle; the overstated significance of demonic types; and the exaggerated importance attached to words and phrases such as "renounce," "bind," and "send to the foot of the Cross." There is no need for Catholics to alter the age-old traditions of an examination of conscience and sincere act of contrition every night, along with frequent reception of the sacrament of penance.

9. How do demons attack people?

Demonic attacks can be divided into ordinary and extraordinary; the ordinary attacks are commonly called temptations. Temptations can come from the world and the flesh, as well as from the devil (*Catechism of the Council of Trent* part IV, petition 6). Temptations of the world include wealth, popularity, and power; temptations of the flesh include sex, food, alcohol, and drugs. The temptations of the devil are intertwined with the other two types: they give added enticement to those sins (*CCC* 2846–54). Temptation by demons is not much different from temptations that come from other people. Just as people can say things to tempt others to sin, so too demons, in a nonverbal way, can give evil thoughts and provoke emotions that can lead to sin.

Exorcists talk about demonic attacks that fall somewhere in between temptation and possession. This is not part of Church teaching; rather it is an acceptable Catholic *opinion*. In the Bible we can see the basis for acknowledging this level of demonic attack. For example, when Jesus saw a woman chronically bent over due to a "spirit of infirmity," he laid his hands on her and cured her (Luke 13:10–16). Jesus said the woman had been "bound" by Satan, but the Gospel does not say she was possessed, and Jesus did not address the demon directly. The infirm woman did not display the signs of possession recorded elsewhere in the Gospels, such as demons shrieking at the sight of Jesus and screaming his name. Therefore it is possible she was suffering from a demonic attack that was less than full-fledged possession.

The two types of attacks that fall into this category between temptation and possession are usually called *oppression* and *obsession*. Demonic *oppression* is often described as an attack that is *external*. The biblical accounts of Job and the woman with the spirit of infirmity are examples of the ways in which demons may attack people physically without actually possessing them. Some exorcists say that in addition to causing physical diseases, demonic oppression may involve attacks on the victims' finances, relationships, and employment. In Job's case, we believe it to be a demonic attack because the Bible states that it is. However, outside of the Bible it would be practically impossible to discern this type of attack. For example, someone might imagine that his financial hardships and strained personal relationships are the result of a demonic attack, when in reality he is simply facing the natural human consequences of an economic recession. But one type of oppression, or external attack, that is clearly demonic is when there is physical activity outside the laws of nature, such as objects moving of their own accord, electrical devices functioning without a power source, or noises or lights that have no earthly source. If such occurrences happen repeatedly in close proximity to a particular person, it is generally called demonic oppression.

Demonic *obsession* usually refers to an attack that is *internal*. A possible biblical example of this is when St. Paul was attacked three times by "a messenger of Satan" (2 Cor. 12:7–9). We don't know what kind of attack it was, but it may have been internal. Exorcists' examples of the internal attacks associated with demonic obsession include the following: evil thoughts that victims cannot stop thinking, spirits that cling to emotional wounds or unhealthy relationships, and evil or frightening dreams. These problems are demonic in a certain way, since Satan is the primary cause of evil in the world, and his demons are always looking for ways to inflict damage on us. However, it would be a mistake to give the devil too much credit for causing such problems, and thereby fail to address the other factors involved. Traumatic experiences, our own sins, and the damage of original sin are all causes of psychological and emotional suffering.

In conformity with the words of Jesus (cf. Matt. 17:18, Mark 1:24), the Catholic Rite of Exorcism refers to demons as being *in* possessed persons, and the process of exorcism as driving the demons *out* of them. However, it should be noted that demons are purely spiritual beings, and therefore do not occupy space as do material objects (CCC 330). The manner in which demons are *in* or *out* of persons (or places) is a matter of philosophical and theological debate, and is not essential in regard to actual cases of possession and exorcism. The important factor is that demons are exerting their power over the bodies of the possessed. The demons are literally in *possession* of the victims' bodies, and are therefore controlling their actions and words.

10. How does a person become possessed?

Exorcists are generally in agreement on how a person becomes possessed by demons. They give three categories of activities and experiences that open a person to demonic possession. As one exorcist said to me, "The darkness is there, waiting to receive an invitation." These three categories are invitations for demonic attacks, though the demons do not always respond by possessing the person. In fact, full-fledged demonic possession is extremely rare, which is why the vast majority of people have never witnessed it.

The first category of behavior that invites demons into one's life is the occult. This includes satanism, the use of tarot cards and the Ouija board, and consulting psychics and mediums. It also includes necromancy, which means trying to consult with spirits of the dead for the sake of learning hidden knowledge or future events. This category is specifically mentioned in the Rite of Exorcism, which instructs the exorcist to command the demons to reveal whether they are in the possessed individual by means of necromancy, or evil signs, or amulets. The exorcist orders the possessed individual to reveal such cursed objects or idols if he has them concealed on his person. If such things were swallowed, the exorcist commands the demons to vomit them out, and he then burns them. This raises the question whether one person can cause another to be possessed through the use of magic, spells, curses, or evil objects. In a certain sense the answer is no, since a human being cannot force demons to possess people. On the other hand, demons may cooperate with evil people, and it is possible for them to possess individuals at the request of such evildoers.

A second, more general opening to demon possession is a *pattern* of sin. This does not mean simply being a sinner, since all humans (except Jesus and Mary) are sinners. Rather, this refers to people who have a habit of serious sin they are attached to and have no intention of stopping. There is a conscious decision to give oneself to the sin, which demons can see as an invitation to their activity.

Being a victim of trauma or abuse is a third category of experience that can open a door to demonic possession. The trauma may include witnessing a murder, suicide, or horrific accident; the abuse may be sexual, physical, or psychological. One exorcist explained that those who go through these experiences can end up living in the dark emotions of anger, rage, resentment, and revenge (*Catholic Exorcists*). He stressed the importance of such victims getting the psychological and spiritual help they need in order to have some degree of healing. If they do not, those emotions can weaken their relationship with God and simultaneously become an opening to a relationship with evil spirits.

This is not to say that every person—or even the majority of persons—who fit these categories are going to become demon-possessed. Possession is extremely rare, even amongst those who partake in these activities or undergo severe trauma. Nevertheless, possession does occur, and it does not happen at random. As one exorcist said, "It's gradual steps. No one wakes up one morning [saying], I'm possessed. This has all taken place over an evolution of a relationship" (*Catholic Exorcists*). It is very foolish for people to establish—even in a small way—a relationship with evil spirits.

There is a difference of opinion amongst exorcists—and amongst faithful priests and Catholic laity—on whether certain elements of pop culture can be an opening to the demonic. Certainly not every book, play, movie, or game that mentions demons is inherently evil. From Dante's *Inferno* to C.S. Lewis' *Screwtape Letters*, the Church has a long history of stories in which the devil is plainly shown to be evil. The debate does not revolve around this type of story, but those that are not clear in their portrayals of good and evil. Does watching a movie or reading a book that shows witchcraft in a positive light constitute an invitation to the devil? Are fantasy games involving spells spiritually dangerous? Some exorcists are quite adamant that Catholics should have nothing to do with these. Yet even they make exceptions; for example, Catholics who object to other books involving magicians are often fans of Tolkien's *Lord of the Rings*. One of the story's main characters (Gandalf) is unquestionably good, though he is a wizard who casts magic spells. Many solid Catholics have read even less reputable stories of magic and witchcraft, apparently without spiritual jeopardy. Ironically, people who are more inclined to show inordinate interest in such topics are precisely the ones who should avoid them. In this way, the question of magic is comparable to that of drinking alcohol: those who can take it or leave it are not at risk, whereas those who have an excessive desire for it should abstain.

11. What are the signs of possession?

The traditional Rite of Exorcism enumerates three specific signs that may accompany demon possession. The first is "ability to speak with some facility in a strange tongue or to understand it when spoken by another." A typical example of this is when the exorcist is performing the rite in Latin and the possessed person, who does not know that language, either mocks the prayers or responds offensively in Latin. The language could be ancient or modern, but it must be a real language, one that is or was spoken by human beings. Incoherent babbling does not count as a sign of demon possession. The rite says that the possessed person must have "some facility," which means it is not enough for him to speak or understand a few phrases that he might have heard at some time. For a true sign of possession, the exorcist must be reasonably certain that the person truly has never learned the language he is using while possessed.

The second sign of demonic possession is the person displaying "knowledge of future and hidden events." Although only God knows the future, demons know much more than human beings do. Through very intelligent and knowledgeable predictions, they can appear to tell the future. As spirits they can travel anywhere in the world instantaneously; they can listen to private conversations and observe private actions; they can communicate with one another about what they see and hear; and they remember all of it. Revealing information about the private life of the exorcist—or one of those assisting him—is a typical example of hidden knowledge, and a clear sign that the person is possessed.

The third sign of demonic possession is the "display of powers which are beyond the subject's age and natural condition." Exorcists say this is typically shown by strength beyond what a person should normally have. This sign can be tricky, because other factors can appear to give individuals strength beyond what is normal. It is astonishing to see how strong people can be when not in their right mind due to drugs, mental disorders, or a fierce rush of emotions. In such instances, people may not care whether they hurt themselves or others, which makes their strength appear all the more abnormal. Another display of power that is beyond human nature is levitation, when a person's body rises from the ground and is suspended in midair. This is a demonstration of the power of an angel—a fallen angel—to move a material body.

The devil cannot perform actual miracles, which by definition are done by the power of God, so instead he carries out mockeries of the truly miraculous. The signs of demon possession illustrate this. As at Pentecost the Holy Spirit inspired the apostles to speak in the many languages of their listeners, so the demons use the vocal cords of possessed individuals to speak languages unknown to them. God revealed to the prophets knowledge of hidden and future events; in their insolence, possessing demons show their knowledge of the past and their shrewd insights into the future. Finally, as Jesus showed power beyond nature by his miraculous cures, the devil demonstrates his power as a (fallen) angel by controlling human bodies and driving them beyond their normal capacity.

The traditional Rite of Exorcism implies that a negative reaction to the sacred is a fourth sign of possession; this sign is stated explicitly in the newer rite. In addition to prayers and Scripture readings, the ritual instructs exorcists to use sacred articles such as holy water, relics, and a crucifix. When he does so, the possessed person may respond in various ways, including: laughing, snorting, howling, spitting, vomiting, convulsing, shouting, screaming, threatening, and even using physical aggression. One difficulty with this sign is that, although it accompanies authentic cases of possession, it may also indicate the lesser demonic attacks called oppression and obsession. In addition, people who mistakenly believe they are possessed often react negatively to the sacred.

After enumerating the three signs, the rite states that the exorcist may take into account "various other indications which, when taken together as a whole, build up the evidence." Since these indications are not specified, exorcists have some latitude in deciding what constitutes a sign of possession. Some exorcists will perform an exorcism only if they see the three signs of possession, whereas others will do so based on alternative signs, such as the following:

- Physical manifestations: convulsions, contortions, facial twitching, total loss of energy
- Deterioration of personal and social life: breakdown in personal relationships, financial struggles, employment problems
- Changes in personality: isolation, difficulty conversing, fascination with the occult
- Effects on consciousness and the senses: nightmares, waking terrors, feeling disconnected from reality, sensing a presence of evil

There is a sharp contrast between the three signs found in the rite and the ones just listed: the latter can have any number of natural causes, whereas the former are more clearly preternatural.

12. What are the risks of confusing mental disorders and demonic activity?

It is possible for someone to suffer simultaneously from a mental disorder and demon possession. This is actually quite reasonable, according to the logic of the devils; being entirely evil, they would have a cruel desire to assault those who are already suffering from a mental disorder. Since no mental disorder can give a person facility in a language he doesn't know or knowledge of hidden events, exorcists who insist upon seeing these signs from the Rite of Exorcism are unlikely to perform an exorcism on someone who is mentally disturbed but not demon-possessed. In contrast, exorcists who consider other signs—such as deterioration in one's personal and social life, changes in personality, and effects on consciousness—may fall into this mistake, since these signs are also symptomatic of certain mental disorders. Such exorcists are aware of this possibility and think the potential benefit of driving out possessing demons is worth the risk. An unnecessary exorcism, they think, harms no one. From a mental health point of view, however, it can certainly be harmful to perform the Rite of Exorcism on individuals suffering from mental problems but not demonic attacks.

If someone consents to be treated as demon-possessed when his actual problems are strictly mental or emotional, he may feel insulted, angry, or abused after the attempted exorcism. Another negative outcome involves people with emotional struggles such as anxiety and depression, who often feel a lack of control over their emotions. If they are erroneously told they are under demonic attack, an unnecessary exorcism can be detrimental by reinforcing the belief that they have no control over their emotions. A similar mistake can occur with those who, as a result of schizophrenia, claim to sense an evil presence in or near them. A wrong diagnosis and an unnecessary exorcism can leave them feeling more hopeless, since even an exorcist could not drive out the evil they think is afflicting them. Further, people with dissociative identity disorder are believed to have a number of different identities or personalities as a result of trauma and abuse. Psychological treatment for this disorder involves gradually helping them to realize that these identities are all part of the same individual person. In the course of a mistaken and unnecessary exorcism, the exorcist might repeatedly address these different personalities as different demons. In doing so, he would reinforce the idea that they are different persons and cause the disorder to be even more ingrained.

As mentioned, it is practically impossible to mistake the dramatic signs of possession—facility in a strange language or knowledge of hidden events—for a mental problem. However, the lower level demonic attacks called oppression and obsession can have signs identical to the symptoms of mental disorders. Again, it is virtually impossible to distinguish in any particular case whether obsessive thoughts, patterns of unhealthy relationships, and nightmares are the result of mental and emotional problems or demonic attacks.

The prudent approach to all such problems is to address both possibilities. For the mental health aspect, those suffering from these struggles should consult a physician and/or a counselor. On the spiritual side, since obsession and oppression are not defined by the Church as calling for the Rite of Exorcism, the usual Catholic practices—frequent Communion and confession, daily prayer, and avoiding the occasions of sin—should be followed faithfully. These spiritual habits are the best means of resisting demonic attacks, and they can also help mental and emotional health. By taking both approaches, one guards against the harm that could result from neglect of one or the other.

13. Do demons ever possess places or things?

The word *possession* refers to demons exerting their power over a human body; *infestation* is the term used when demons exert their power over a particular place or thing. The Rite of Exorcism has a set of prayers specifically intended for cases of infestation. Entitled the "Exorcism of Satan and the Fallen Angels," these are sometimes called the "Prayers of Leo XIII" for the pope who added them to the rite.

The only clear example of demonic infestation in the Bible is the incident involving the possessed man in the country of the Gerasenes (Mark 5:1–20). When Jesus drove the demons from the man, he allowed them to enter into a herd of pigs. Demons possessing the bodies of animals is one type of infestation. Another type is when demons attack a specific city or community. Probably the most well-known type of infestation is when demons cause a disturbance in a particular place such as a house or other building. The common term for this is to say that a place is *haunted*.

Haunted houses are commonly believed to be inhabited by the spirits of dead human beings. The angels and saints in heaven can speak to people if God wills, but there is no reason for them to disturb a house or other building. The same can be said of the souls in purgatory, or the Poor Souls, as they are sometimes called. The only reason for souls to be in purgatory is to go through some kind of suffering in order to be purified of the sins they committed during their lives on earth. The Bible says that we can help the Poor Souls to pay for their sins by offering prayers and sacrifices for them (2 Macc. 12:32–46). It is possible that souls in purgatory may do their penance by helping people in this world, or that they may appear to people to ask that prayers and sacrifices be offered for them. But it is difficult to see how the Poor Souls would be purged of their sins by making noises, flickering lights, and moving objects around a house. In regard to human souls in hell, the Church does not have a definitive teaching as to whether they can return to earth as part of their punishment, so there may actually be places that are haunted by the dead.

There are creatures that have the capability and motivation to haunt houses: the devils. They have the ability to do all the things we think of in connection with haunted houses: make noises, move objects, trigger air movements, and cause the temperature to drop. Demons can appear in the form of human beings, such as someone who once lived in a given location, or even one of our own family members. The reason why devils would haunt a house is simple: they will do anything to draw people away from God, so it fits their agenda to get people more interested in ghosts than in the Faith. Consider the interest in this topic, as seen by the number of television programs and books that deal with it. By getting people to focus on meaningless spiritual diversions like haunted houses, the devil hopes to distract them from truly important spiritual realities such as sin and the state of their own souls. Similarly, people who give attention to such demonic activity can allow fear of the devil to loom larger in their lives than their faith and hope in Christ.

Anyone who thinks demons may be infesting his house should take two steps. The first is the more important and more difficult: he should examine his moral and spiritual life, acknowledge and repent of his sins, and make a priority of reforming his life in line with the teachings of Christ. The other step is to contact a priest and ask him to bless the house. If in doing so the priest witnesses any preternatural manifestations, such as objects moving of their own accord or inexplicable noises, he may ask his bishop to authorize a priest to come to the house and perform the section of the Rite of Exorcism for infestation.

The bishop may also authorize a priest to perform that part of the ritual over an animal if it displays unnatural abilities. Although very rare, possession of animals is nonetheless possible, as in the case of the Gerasene demoniac. There are stories of houses being haunted by animal spirits, but animals do not have immortal souls; there is nothing left of them when they die. Since there are no souls of terriers, tarantulas, or tuna fish in the afterlife, we can rule out the possibility that houses are haunted by them or any other animal. The devils, however, are certainly capable of appearing in the form of any creature; again, in an attempt to stir interest in nonsensical matters, they may fool people into thinking a place is haunted by an animal spirit.

14. What is the difference between exorcism and deliverance?

The word exorcism comes from the Greek word *ex-orkizo*, which means *to adjure*, or in other words, to charge, bind, or command earnestly and solemnly. The Church uses the word "exorcism" in several ways. People commonly think of the word in relation to a priest performing the Church's official Rite of Exorcism. This is done when a bishop is presented with evidence that convinces him a person is possessed by demons; he appoints an exorcist, a priest he sanctions to do the rite.

The word "exorcism" is used in a more specific way in both the Rite of Exorcism and in the traditional (extraordinary form) Rite of Baptism. In these rituals the word refers specifically to when the priest speaks directly to the devils, ordering them to depart. There are numerous instances in the Gospels of this meaning of the word "exorcism," such as the following:

There was in their synagogue a man with an unclean spirit; and he cried out, "What have you to do with us, Jesus of Nazareth? Have you come to destroy us? I know who you are, the Holy One of God." But Jesus rebuked him, saying, "Be silent, and come out of him!" And the unclean spirit, convulsing him and crying with a loud voice, came out of him. And they were all amazed, so that they questioned among themselves, saying, "What is this? A new teaching! With authority he commands even the unclean spirits, and they obey him" (Mark 1:23–27).

The Rite of Exorcism includes three specific exorcisms—three sections in which the priest specifically commands the demons to depart. For example: "I cast you out, unclean spirit, along with every satanic power of the enemy, every specter from hell, and all your fell companions; in the name of our Lord Jesus Christ. Begone and stay far from this creature of God." In the Rite of Baptism the priest also addresses the demons directly three times. These are called *simple* or *minor* exorcisms, one of which begins: "I exorcise thee, unclean spirit, in the name of the Father, and of the Son, and of the Holy Spirit, that you go out and depart from this servant of God."

A more general meaning of the word exorcism is found in the *Catechism*: "When the Church asks publicly and authoritatively in the name of Jesus Christ that a person or object be protected against the power of the Evil One and withdrawn from his dominion, it is called exorcism" (1673). Here the words are not commands that demons depart, but are prayers asking God that they do so. The modern (ordinary form) Rite of Baptism uses this type of exorcism: "Almighty and ever-living God, you sent your only Son into the world to cast out the power of Satan, spirit of evil, to rescue man from the kingdom of darkness, and bring him into the splendor of your kingdom of light."

All of the above points about exorcism should be understood in sharp contrast to the practice known as *deliverance*. The Church does not define deliverance, does not have a ritual for it, and does not have sanctioned ministers for it. Therefore, those who assert themselves as practitioners of deliverance are inventing their own definition of what it means, how it is to be done, and who is to do it. Deliverance commonly refers to the practice, whether through prayers to God or commands aimed at demons, of breaking the lower-level demonic attacks known as temptation, oppression, and obsession. It is, of course, a good thing to pray to God each day for protection against the devil, as we do each time we say "deliver us from evil" in the Lord's Prayer. It is more questionable whether people should, as a general practice, address devils directly, as in the following: "In the name of Jesus I break the power of every evil spirit that (person's name) has renounced, and any related spirit, and I command them to leave now in the name of Jesus." The Church does not forbid the practice, but neither is there any Church ritual in which anyone issues commands to demons other than authorized exorcists (in the Rite of Exorcism) and priests or deacons (in the minor exorcisms of baptism). One would think that if the practice were commendable, there would be at least one example of it in Church ritual.

Deliverance ministry, as currently practiced among some Catholics, has a curious history. There is a branch of Protestantism called Pentecostalism, the adherents of which believe that they frequently receive supernatural gifts from God such as miraculous healing powers, knowledge of other people's thoughts or personal history, and prophetic messages about the future. Another important aspect of this spirituality is a belief in one's awareness of the activity of demons and one's power to expel them.

In the late 1960s, some Catholics began to bring Pentecostal spirituality into the Church. There was no opportunity, however, to drive out demons in the same dramatic fashion as their Pentecostal counterparts, since Catholics believe that—in addition to authorized exorcisms—prayer and the sacraments are the strongest means of fighting demons. Therefore, as they adopted Pentecostal beliefs in relation to other supernatural gifts, these Catholics also began to imitate the Pentecostal practice of deliverance. They added Catholic aspects such as asking the help of the Virgin Mary, the angels, and the saints. As long as they do not claim to be performing exorcisms, these practices generally do not contradict Church teaching or violate Church law.

At the same time, Catholics should be aware that the Church does not officially recognize any special abilities, methods, or made-up rituals used by those involved in so-called deliverance ministry. For example, holding out one's hand in order to "pray over" a person for protection against demons is no more authoritative than folding one's hands and "praying for" them; asking to be "covered by the blood of Christ" is not as powerful as receiving his body and blood in Holy Communion; using the phrase "I renounce" in reference to one's past sins is not superior to a careful examination of conscience, sincere contrition, and a firm purpose of amendment; and the grace of the sacrament of penance is certainly greater.

15. What does the exorcist do?

Exorcist is simply the title of a priest who has been chosen by his bishop to perform an exorcism. The Rite of Exorcism says an exorcist should have the virtues of piety, prudence, integrity, constancy, and humility. In designating a priest with these qualities, the bishop may assign him to perform one exorcism, or he may appoint him to be the exorcist for the diocese. A bishop may give that assignment for a certain period, such as a three-year term, or for an indefinite period of time. He may renew the assignment as often as desired, or he may end it at any time. A bishop may require the exorcist to request permission each time he performs an exorcism, or he may tell the exorcist to use his own judgment and perform exorcisms at his own discretion. If a bishop faced with a case of demonic possession does not have in mind one of his own priests, he can contact another bishop and ask that bishop to send an exorcist to perform the exorcism.

The Rite of Exorcism states that the exorcist should study the subject of exorcism by examining cases and reading approved authors. Some priests have no particular expertise or training before they become exorcists; others have assisted an exorcist periodically, or even had a sort of apprenticeship with an exorcist. Some were involved in so-called deliverance and claim to have seen demonic attacks through this ministry before they were appointed exorcists. In recent years, conferences and seminars on the topics of demon possession and exorcism have been held, and priests might attend one or more of these before being assigned to perform an exorcism. Exorcists agree that, as in most areas of life, experience in the process is a valuable asset.

Exorcists stress the importance of their own spiritual and moral life, being consistent in prayer, receiving the sacrament of penance (confession), and avoiding the occasions of sin, especially mortal sin. When offering Mass on the day of an exorcism, they specifically pray for the possessed individual and may ask the help of the saint whose feast is being celebrated. The Rite of Exorcism indicates another means of preparation; it references the time when the apostles asked

Jesus why they were not able to drive out a particular demon, and he responded by telling them that kind could be driven out only by prayer and fasting (Matt. 17:21). The rite instructs the exorcist "to avail himself of these two means above all for imploring the divine assistance in expelling demons . . . and not only himself, but let him induce others, as far as possible, to do the same." Exorcists are often in close contact with religious sisters who, from their convents, on the day of the exorcism, join their prayers for the specific intention of driving out the demons.

The exorcism ceremony itself consists of prayers, Gospel readings, psalms, commands to the demons, and the use of holy water, relics, and the crucifix. While the exorcist is performing the ritual, the demons may display the signs of possession with greater intensity. These signs are all physically associated with the bodies of the victims: their voices are used to speak strange languages and reveal hidden knowledge, and their bodies show unnatural power and react to the sacred. During the exorcism, the devils may also cause unnatural occurrences outside the body of the possessed person, such as detached voices and noises, foul smells, objects moving, electronic devices turning on and off, and a drastic drop in temperature. As frightening as these sound, exorcists say there is no need to be afraid during an exorcism, and those present should not give in to fear. One exorcist called these manifestations "cheap parlor tricks," and another called them "noise and distractions."[2] Although they say these goings-on can be alarming at first, they become easier to ignore as the exorcist performs more exorcisms over time.

Exorcists are unanimous in recognizing the strength of the Blessed Virgin Mary against the devil. Several times during the course of the rite, the exorcist invokes her name, as in the following line: "The exalted Virgin Mary, Mother of God, commands you, who in her lowliness crushed your proud head from the first moment of her Immaculate Conception." The ritual tells the exorcist that "it will also help to say devoutly and often over the afflicted person the Our Father, Hail Mary, and the Creed." It is no coincidence that these are the prayers of the rosary, which exorcists consider to be particularly powerful and especially hated by the devils.

16. Does exorcism always work?

Some exorcists report that it typically takes between one and ten sessions of the Rite of Exorcism to expel the demons completely from a possessed person. They also say that as long as the possessed person is not reverting, between sessions, to the same habits of sin that led to the possession in the first place, the exorcism ritual is essentially 100 percent effective in driving out the demons. Other exorcists, however, describe doing exorcism sessions every month or more for a period of years and yet never successfully expelling the devil from the possessed person. It is legitimate to ask whether the latter cases actually involve people suffering from mental disorders instead of possession; if the exorcism sessions were done without clear evidence of the three signs from the rite, the question becomes even more substantial.

The Rite of Exorcism states: "Once in a while, after [the demons] are already recognized, they conceal themselves and leave the body practically free from every molestation, so that the victim believes himself completely delivered. Yet the exorcist may not desist until he sees the signs of deliverance." Exorcists say one obvious indication that the demons are gone is that the three signs named explicitly in the rite (speaking in a strange language, knowledge of hidden or future events, physical power beyond nature), as well as the implied fourth sign (negative reaction to the sacred), have stopped manifesting for an extended period of time. Exorcists also look for an abiding sense of peace to come over the possessed person, which may indicate that the demons have departed. Demons may shriek when driven out, as seen both in the Gospels (cf. Luke 4:33–41) and in reports by exorcists. A more subtle indication that may accompany the exodus of the devil is a peculiar exhaling from the nose and/or mouth.

The exorcist may order the demons to give a specific sign when they are driven out, as in the following description:

The command was given as a sign of departure to say, "Hail Mary, full of grace." Then the demon responded by saying, "Grace thou full." Scrambled the words, never said the name of the Blessed Mother, but scrambled the words around and then laughed. And then the command [was] given in the name of Christ to say the words in order; the demon was commanded to say them. The demon then said, "Hail Mary, full of grace," and then shrieked. Then the person—just like that—said, "How are you doing, Father?"[3]

After a successful exorcism, an exorcist generally waits for the freed individual to contact him for follow-up conversations, encouraging him to do so for about a year. If the exorcist believes the person is also suffering from a mental or emotional disorder, he will encourage him to continue seeing a counselor or psychologist. When the exorcist stops hearing from him, he presumes the individual is doing well. After being freed from the demons, it is certainly possible for a victim to resume his old sinful habits. Invoking the words of Jesus, the Rite of Exorcism instructs the exorcist to warn victims about this: "Finally, after the possessed one has been freed, let him be admonished to guard himself carefully against falling into sin, so as to afford no opportunity to the evil spirit of returning, lest the last state of that man become worse than the former." Apparently a second case of possession is rare, since those who have been possessed are usually eager to make the changes necessary to avoid further demonic influence.

In order to facilitate the necessary change in life, the exorcist admonishes the formerly possessed person to establish a solid moral and spiritual life along the following lines. First, the individual should work on the areas that opened the door to demonic possession in the first place. Occult activities such as satanism, witchcraft, and use of the Ouija board must be abandoned, as should consultations with palm readers, psychics, and horoscopes. Steps should be taken to overcome habits of serious sin such as drug or alcohol abuse and sexual promiscuity. These sinful habits should be replaced by good spiritual habits. Catholics should establish a daily prayer life including, for example, Scripture reading, the rosary, and use of holy water; they should attend Mass every week and go to confession regularly. Non-Catholics should likewise have some kind of daily prayer life and weekly church attendance.

After driving the "legion" of devils from the possessed man in the country of the Gerasenes, Jesus told him: "Go home to your friends, and tell them how much the Lord has done for you, and how he has had mercy on you" (Mark 5:19). Similarly, those who are freed from demonic possession should try to restore any good relationships they may have abandoned, especially with their family and their faith community.

17. Is there any connection between demons and witchcraft, Ouija boards, and psychics?

Witchcraft is not a formal, structured belief system. As one practitioner explained, "I follow a predominately Celtic witch/Tantric path. As time passes, I find myself increasingly drawing upon the wisdom and beliefs of other spiritual paths. . . . When asked I'll tell you I'm a witch; I also consider myself a Wiccan and perhaps part shaman because I utilize and blend aspects of them all."[4] This statement represents a typical amalgam of beliefs that a witch might have: "Celtic witch" indicates Irish beliefs before the time of St. Patrick (c. 400); Wicca is a twentieth-century Western European paganism; Tantra is a form of Hinduism, based in India; and a shaman originally indicated a spiritual leader and healer in northern Asia, though the word is now used for such a practitioner anywhere in the world. Seeing as all of these influences have shaped the outlook of just one witch, clearly there is no way to define witchcraft as practiced by all who claim the title.

But Wicca/witchcraft certainly excludes Christianity: it is virtually impossible to find a self-declared witch who also professes belief in the Triune God, the Incarnation, and salvation through the Crucifixion and bodily Resurrection of Christ.

A common theme amongst witches is the emphasis on nature as good in itself and possessing power that may be tapped into. As a result, it is common for witches not only to worship nature, but also to believe that certain rituals called spells can control nature. It is vital to see that this view is the opposite of the Catholic faith: nature is not good and powerful in itself, but is an expression of the all-good, all-powerful God, whom alone Catholics worship. Catholic prayer, likewise, is the opposite of witches' spells: rather than trying to exert control, prayer recognizes that God is in control and implores his help, his blessings, and his mercy.

The Ouija board is actually nothing but wood, paper, and plastic (though there are now virtual Ouija boards on the internet); it has no inherent power. It was invented in the 1890s, a time when spiritualism, or the attempt to communicate with spirits of the dead, was popular in the United States. But the creator of the Ouija board was perhaps less sinister than cynical: he was a businessman who thought of a way to cash in on the unfortunate spiritualist craze. He made up the face of the board, which is mostly letters, along with the words "yes" and "no" (apparently for spirits desiring to give terser answers). He then found a few financial backers, and the Ouija board has been selling ever since. Players rest their hands on the plastic piece, which then—allegedly powered by spirits or other mysterious forces—moves around the board to spell out answers or advice.

Psychic abilities generally refer to unexplained powers of the mind such as perceiving others' thoughts or communicating one's own, acquiring knowledge without the use of the five senses, and mentally seeing the past or future. Certainly God can reveal such information to someone, so the case has been made that these abilities do not contradict Church teaching. But prophets who speak under divine inspiration always have God's law as their primary message; revealing hidden knowledge or foretelling future events is incidental. In modern culture, the typical practices of psychics are blatantly immoral, as in the case of the street-corner psychic charging ten dollars to tell customers their future or to contact their deceased relatives.

Where does the devil fit into all of this? There is only one good way to communicate with the spirit world, and that is through prayer. We pray to God; we ask his angels and saints to pray for us (as we also ask people in this world for prayers); we pray for the souls in purgatory. Worship of anyone or anything other than the one true God is seriously sinful; other gods—whether they are thought to be deities, nature spirits, or a sentient spirit of the world itself—do not exist. There is no moral way to communicate with the spirit world other than prayer. People interested in contacting spirits in other ways are not going to interact with good spiritual beings. The only ones who respond to such attempts are demons, and they do so for their own purposes: by giving people the illusion of mysterious powers, the devil attempts to draw them away from God and to get others to follow them. Recall that angels—including fallen angels—have a vast knowledge of the material world, extending from the beginning of time to the present; further, by seeing and analyzing what is happening in the present, they can make shrewd predictions about the future. With these powers, devils can communicate nonverbally, through mental concepts, and thereby give people knowledge beyond their natural ability. Witches, Ouija board players, and psychics can be fooled into thinking their practices are authentic, when in reality they are being played as fools by the devil. Similarly, the devil can manipulate physical matter, so a witch who thinks she can control nature, or a shaman who thinks he is working a healing spell, may simply be a victim of the devil's deception.

18. What prayers and practices can people adopt for protection against demons?

Many Christians have their preferred prayers for protection against demons, and as long as there is nothing in such prayers that contradicts the Faith, they are all good. But there is an unfortunate tendency among some in the Church to claim certain "deliverance prayers" have special power against the devil. In fact, the Church has no such prayers, so Catholics should not be awed by the word "deliverance" when it is attached to someone's favorite prayer.

The Rite of Exorcism provides the Church's most powerful prayers and practices for driving out demons. Though only a priest specifically authorized by his bishop may perform the rite in its entirety, it contains numerous instructions and prayers of which all Catholics are encouraged to avail themselves for protection against the devil:

- The exorcist "is to be distinguished for his piety, prudence, and integrity of life . . . constancy, and humility." Practicing these virtues is a powerful bulwark against demonic influence.
- Quoting Jesus' words from Matthew's Gospel, the rite tells the exorcist to practice prayer and fasting, and to induce others to do the same.
- The exorcist is instructed to go to confession and offer Mass before beginning the exorcism ritual; if possible, in between exorcism sessions, the possessed person is also to receive the sacraments of

penance and Holy Communion. Frequent reception of these sacraments is the greatest means given to Catholics to increase sanctifying grace in our souls, thereby helping us to resist the temptations and other assaults of the devil.

- The possessed person "should entreat [God] with firm faith and in all humility. And if he is all the more grievously tormented, he ought to bear this patiently, never doubting the divine assistance." In the midst of any trial—of demonic origin or otherwise—all are exhorted to exercise the virtues of faith, humility, and patience.

- The exorcist is to have a crucifix at hand. He begins the ceremony by tracing the sign of the cross on himself, the possessed person, and those assisting; he then sprinkles holy water on all present. Catholics should make the sign of the cross devoutly and frequently. They should have a blessed crucifix in their homes, and it is a good practice to cross oneself with holy water in the morning and at night. Those who cannot have a crucifix in the workplace can keep a bottle of holy water there and sprinkle it daily.

- The first prayer in the rite is the Litany of the Saints. In addition to saying this prayer for help against demons, Catholics should ask their patron saints and guardian angels for protection every day.

- As Jesus quoted Scripture to drive off the devil, so the exorcist, while performing the exorcism ritual, reads numerous Gospel passages and Psalms. Reading the Bible daily is a good spiritual habit for all Christians, and a solid means of keeping demons at bay.

- The exorcist is told "it will also help to say devoutly and often over the afflicted person the Our Father, Hail Mary, and the Creed." By praying the rosary devoutly and often, Catholics are availing themselves of all three of these. Just as Jesus has a special love for his mother, so demons have a special hatred for her, and exorcists strongly recommend praying the rosary for her protection against the devil.

- The ritual includes a longer version of the prayer to St. Michael the archangel. Catholics can invoke his assistance by praying it in the shorter form used for many years at the end of Low Mass.

A number of prayers with official standing in the Church include an invocation for protection against the devil. One is the Litany of St. Joseph, approved by Pope St. Pius X. It honors the foster father of our Lord with numerous invocations, including: "St. Joseph, terror of demons, pray for us." Another prayer is the Chaplet of St. Michael, which was approved by Blessed Pope Pius IX. It asks each of the nine choirs of angels for a particular assistance; the choir of powers is specifically asked to intercede for "protection against the snares and temptations of the devil."

Many Catholics wear the St. Benedict Medal or keep it on their person or in their home. Designed by the monks of Benedict's ancient monastery of Monte Cassino, it includes Latin initials for the following prayers of protection against demons:

- May the holy cross be for me a light! (*Crux sacra sit mihi lux.*)
- Let not the dragon be my overlord! (*Non draco sit mihi dux.*)
- Begone, Satan! Suggest not to me your vanities! (*Vade retro Satana! Nunquam suade mihi vana!*)
- The drink you offer is evil! Drink that poison yourself! (*Sunt mala quae libas! Ipse venena bibas!*)

Likewise, a night prayer from the Liturgy of the Hours concludes as follows: "Lord, we beg you to visit this house and banish from it all the deadly power of the enemy. May your holy angels dwell here to keep us in peace, and may your blessing be upon us always. We ask this through Christ our Lord. Amen."

19. What should a person do if he thinks someone he knows may be possessed?

Before contacting an exorcist, a person who thinks he or someone he knows might be possessed by demons should first talk to his pastor or a priest in any nearby parish. If the priest agrees that it may be a case of possession, he can contact his bishop. If the priest does not think it is a case of possession, but the person concerned still believes that it is, the latter can talk to another priest, contact the bishop's office directly, or call the diocesan exorcist. Some bishops allow their exorcists to be quite open about their role, in which case people may find an exorcist's name on a diocesan website, see a notice that he is going to give a talk or a retreat, or hear about him by word of mouth.

Exorcists say they are frequently contacted by people who think that they themselves, or someone they know, might be possessed by demons. These people might call to make an appointment to speak with the exorcist, though sometimes they come to see him unannounced. Oftentimes they have already talked to a priest who then referred them to the exorcist. Exorcists involved in deliverance and healing services meet many people at such gatherings who believe they are being attacked by demons.

If someone walks into the exorcist's office and exhibits the three signs given in the Rite of Exorcism, it is fairly clear that he is possessed. But such a case is uncommon. The person may be having mental or emotional problems, such as: feeling disconnected from reality, the sensation of a presence of evil, or hearing voices telling them to commit crimes. He may have had a series of crises or tragedies: illness, injury, or the death of a loved one; the break-up of a close relationship; the loss of employment or some other financial calamity. He may have experienced inexplicable frightening occurrences, including: strange noises and voices coming from empty rooms; objects mysteriously moved or disturbed; and mechanical or electronic devices starting or stopping of their own accord.

The exorcist begins each case with the presumption that those who come to see him are not possessed. *Natural* causes are those that follow God's usual laws of nature, so they offer the first possible explanation to consider; only after such an explanation is eliminated should an exorcist look to the preternatural. As opposed to the *supernatural* works of God, which go beyond the laws of nature as we understand them, *preternatural* works are deceptions of the devil, who has powers beyond those of human beings, but (obviously) not equal to those of God.

Those who contact exorcists for help have often already made up their minds that they are possessed. The exorcist tells them he wants to help relieve their suffering, and in order to do so, he must try to find out what is behind their problems. The cause could be spiritual, physical, mental, emotional, or a combination thereof. If after the initial interview the exorcist thinks the cause is physical, he may consult or recommend a physician. If he thinks the cause is mental or emotional, he may consult or recommend a counselor or psychologist. In order to determine the cause, the exorcist may ask questions touching on a range of topics, including the following:

- Age, marital status, home life, family background
- History of trauma, abuse, mental disorders, substance abuse, psychotropic medicines
- Religious affiliation, church attendance, prayer life
- Involvement with Ouija board, Tarot cards, palm reading, psychics, Wicca, etc.
- Books read or movies seen about the devil
- Previous experience with deliverance or exorcism

Prayer is an important part of the initial interview. Depending upon the individual exorcist, he may use prayers of his own choosing, or he may say some of the prayers found in the Rite of Exorcism. Before commencing the full Rite of Exorcism, he may consult another priest, ideally another exorcist. But if the exorcist sees convincing evidence of demon possession from the start, he may proceed immediately with the Rite of Exorcism, which is done in a sacred place such as a church or chapel. There should be a few other people present to pray and to assist the exorcist in case the possessed person becomes physically combative. Exorcists prefer to have another priest present, but this is not always possible or practical.

20. What is the role of guardian angels?

"Beside each believer stands an angel as protector and shepherd leading him to life." This is how St. Basil, quoted in the *Catechism* (336), described the role of the guardian angels. Obviously, God does not need the assistance of the angels; he is capable of taking care of people without them. But in his wisdom God has seen fit to assign angels to watch over human beings. Perhaps because Lucifer, the leader of the fallen angels, led human beings to their downfall, it is appropriate that other angels take part in leading people to salvation. Another reason is that human beings, in their weakness, can take comfort in knowing that they each have an angel specifically designated by God to watch over them.

There are differing opinions regarding when a person's guardian angel is assigned to him. St. Anselm thought the assignment took place at the time of *ensoulment*, when one's body and soul are created, more commonly referred to as *conception*. St. Jerome speculated that only Christians had guardian angels, receiving them when they were baptized. St. Thomas Aquinas thought people received their own guardian angel at birth; perhaps the mother's angel, he reasoned, watched over the unborn child until he left the womb and his own guardian was given to him.

There are many scriptural references to people being protected by angels. In the book of the prophet

Daniel, the three Israelites who refuse to worship a golden idol are cast into a fiery furnace. They survive without even the smell of smoke touching their clothes, thanks to the protection of an angel. In the book of Tobit, Tobit is cured of blindness by the archangel Raphael, who also protects Tobit's son Tobias from the demon Asmodeus. In the Acts of the Apostles, St. Peter is freed from his chains and from prison by an angel. When Jesus, in the Gospel of Luke, endured the agony in the garden of Gethsemane, "there appeared to him an angel from heaven, strengthening him" (22:43). As God the Son, he did not need an angel, but Jesus was also human; this event shows that angels give people strength in times of suffering.

In addition to guarding individuals, angels protect nations, cities, and even parishes. An angel helped lead the Israelites out of slavery in Egypt, and the book of the prophet Daniel names the archangel Michael as the guardian of the nation of Israel. During the time of the prophet Isaiah, an angel protected the city of Jerusalem from an imminent invasion by the Assyrians: "the angel of the Lord went forth, and slew a hundred and eighty-five thousand in the camp of the Assyrians; and when men arose early in the morning, behold, these were all dead bodies" (Isa. 37:36). The book of Revelation mentions angels of churches in particular cities, but since these are sometimes reprimanded for their faults, the word "angel" in this context seems to refer to the bishop of the city. Nevertheless, there is a pious belief that every parish has its own guardian angel; for example, the archives of St. Columba Church in Ottawa, Illinois, reveal that the painting of an angel above the altar depicts the guardian angel of the parish.

In a Vatican document approved by Pope St. John Paul II ("Directory on Popular Piety and the Liturgy," 2001), the practice of assigning names to angels was discouraged as a deviation from authentic spiritual piety. There are several reasons why doing so would be inappropriate. First, angels were created at the beginning of the world, so it is absurd to think that after many eons of time, a human being can suddenly give a name to an angel. Furthermore, assigning a name implies that the one giving it has authority over the one receiving it, as when parents name their children. Human beings are assisted and protected by angels, but that does not mean humans have authority over them. Finally, some people claim that they can learn the name of their guardian angel by praying for it to be revealed. This is essentially the same as assigning a name to an angel: there is no reason to believe that the name the person decides upon is truly the name of the angel. Just as people generally refer to their parents as "Mom" and "Dad," the traditional practice is to refer to one's angel simply as "Guardian Angel."

About the Author

Fr. Mike Driscoll is a priest of the Diocese of Peoria, Illinois. He was ordained in 1992, has been pastor of several parishes, and is currently serving as chaplain of St. Elizabeth's Medical Center in Ottawa, Illinois. He has a B.A. in economics from the University of Illinois, an M.A. in moral theology from Mount St. Mary's Seminary, and a Ph.D. in counselor education and supervision from Regent University. His book, *Demons, Deliverance, and Discernment*, is published by Catholic Answers Press. He can be contacted through his website: peterinchains.org.

Endnotes

1 *De Coelesti Hierarchia* 14.
2 Driscoll, Mike. "How Catholic Exorcists Distinguish between Demonic Possession and Mental Disorders." PhD diss., Regent University, 2013.
3 Ibid.
4 "Witchcraft, Wicca and Paganism: Frequently Asked Questions," www.wicca.com.